DEDICATION

This book is dedicated to my best buddies, Jake and Miranda. Thank you for the ideas you have contributed, they definitely made my book worth the read.

Table of Contents

Mastering Body Language

Understanding Human Behavior To Read And Send Non-Verbal Messages

By: Ronald Young

9781635012736

PUBLISHERS NOTES

Disclaimer – Speedy Publishing LLC

This publication is intended to provide helpful and informative material. It is not intended to diagnose, treat, cure, or prevent any health problem or condition, nor is intended to replace the advice of a physician. No action should be taken solely on the contents of this book. Always consult your physician or qualified health-care professional on any matters regarding your health and before adopting any suggestions in this book or drawing inferences from it.

The author and publisher specifically disclaim all responsibility for any liability, loss or risk, personal or otherwise, which is incurred as a consequence, directly or indirectly, from the use or application of any contents of this book.

Any and all product names referenced within this book are the trademarks of their respective owners. None of these owners have sponsored, authorized, endorsed, or approved this book.

Always read all information provided by the manufacturers' product labels before using their products. The author and publisher are not responsible for claims made by manufacturers.

This book was originally printed before 2014. This is an adapted reprint by Speedy Publishing LLC with newly updated content designed to help readers with much more accurate and timely information and data.

Speedy Publishing LLC

40 E Main Street, Newark, Delaware, 19711

Contact Us: 1-888-248-4521

Website: http://www.speedypublishing.co

REPRINTED Paperback Edition: 9781635012736:

Manufactured in the United States of America

Chapter 1- Talking Without Words: Interpreting Body Language

There are many form of communication and sometimes a person's body language can actually indicate more things than the spoken word. Learning to understand body language can be very beneficial both in the work environment as well as on a more personal front. Body language reveals personal feelings and reactions to other people's feelings. However is has yet to be proven to be a science form and is not a real indicator to anything as it can be and is often manipulated.

Most powerful people use this form of the unspoken word to make judgment calls which have proven to be a very effective way of getting and giving information. Some quarters qualify any and all movements in the body to be categorized as body movement; while others go even further to say that even breathing techniques fall in this category too.

When meeting someone for the first time, it is often a benefit to be able to read their body language signals to assess either the person or situation.

However again it may not be the best way to form an opinion because as mentioned earlier, body language can be manipulated. The art of body language is constantly being exchanged and interpreted between people on different levels of alternative communication.

While you are reading the body language of another person, that other person is already reading your non-verbal cues. People who make it a habit of reading body language sign always have the advantage over any situation the thus having some knowledge on this subject would be good.

The Everyday Uses of Body Language

We use body language every day in our lives to get our message across, to achieve positive feedback in our lives, and to get whatever we want. We use this language all the time, but we may not be aware of it. Moreover, this language doesn't only involve the mouth but the whole body as well. Could you even imagine the awesome power of applying it?

With it, you'll be able to interpret other people's inner emotions even if they're not directly expressing it. You'll also be able to modify your behavior to fit the situation. You'll get them to like and trust you. What words cannot do, body language can. In this chapter, we shall explore the various body gestures or movements conveyed by people in different scenarios.

Chapter 2- Body Language that Relay Positive Messages

Body Language that Greets

Everyone knows waving at another person or shaking their hand is a way of greeting however, there are many other forms of greeting body language used that you may not be aware of. Greeting body language can be used as a secret signal passed between individuals to indicate a type of unity. For example, many gangs have a secret handshake ritual or hand gesture that they use to show their commonality. Grade school children often have their secret little club handshakes as well. Depending on the culture you were raised under, some forms of greeting body language may not be acceptable or may even be considered as an insult.

It is said that you can tell a lot about a person through their handshake however, this is questionable as it all depends on the type of day the person is having and several other factors. A firm handgrip in a handshake is meant to show confidence where as a limp wrist with a light grip is thought to show timidity. However, elderly women especially can lose their grip and have a light grasp so this reasoning is not always the case. The double grip hand shake where not only is the extender shaking the hand but with their other hand gripping the persons elbow or encompassing the others hands between both of theirs is meant to show dominance. However, there are several people who, while shaking the hand of someone to whom they are truly grateful will encompass the persons hand in both of theirs to show sincerity.

Other body language greeting signs thought to be a gesture of dominance are shaking another's hand with the palm down, whereas the palm up shows submission and palms sideways show equality. Extended handshakes where one person makes it difficult for another to end the greeting is also a sign of dominance. If you pay attention to photographs of politicians or of people in authority positions, handshake photos will be taken with the individuals standing shoulder to shoulder with their arm/hand stretched out across their front to greet the others hand. The dominant person will stand to the left of the other person, shaking with the right hand, so that when the picture is taken it is their back of the hand that appears visible in the picture.

Other forms of greeting through hand body language is the "high five" where two people slap hands in the air, tapping fronts of fists or a touch as a person walks by another at a party to show acknowledgement. Other forms of greeting body language are in the form of honor, such as the salute where the hand is brought up towards the forehead or a brim of a hat and back down to the side again. The military use salutes to show respect to those in higher ranks. The boy scouts also have their own special salute. The raising of the hand to the heart when reciting the Pledge of Allegiance is another form of honor salute. Bowing can also show honor or it can show appreciation or thanks such as at the end of a performance. In Japan, if you do not bow at a greeting it is a form of disrespect.

Hugging and kissing are also other forms of greeting body language but should be used under advisement. Greeting a person you do not know with a hug or a kiss could wind you up in a world of trouble. Society is more accepting of women hugging other women in a greeting than they are men hugging one another unless closely related. When a hug becomes more of a body grind, it has gone way past that of a greeting and can border on sexual harassment or even assault if one is not a willing recipient. In some cultures, it is expected to greet another with a kiss, such as the cheek-to-cheek kiss done in France and it can be socially acceptable and expected to be done by either gender to either gender. Greeting kisses are short like a peck on the lips or the cheek of another individual. Greeting a friend may involve a hug while at the same time administering a kiss to the lips or the cheek. Any kiss of any length and on the lips, with open or closed mouth is considered more of a romantic kiss, no longer a greeting.

One can read a person's greeting approach by their facial expressions as well. A frown would be a good indicator that something is wrong, whereas a tensed face with clenched jaw should indicate to you that the person is quite upset or angry at you. A smiling face will indicate that the person is happy to see you whereas a blank facial affect can indicate that the person couldn't care less about you or that you are present. When you see another person squeezing their eyebrows together, it is more than likely they are trying to recall your name before approaching you. This is a great time to go up, remind them politely what your name is and greet them with a friendly handshake. Other forms of body language greetings are tipping the hat as a form of acknowledgement and rubbing noses as in an Eskimo kiss.

Body Language that is Open to All Positive Vibes

Open body language generally expresses relaxation or higher comfort form. Open arms and hands express the persons desire not to hide anything from another as they are relaxed in their current situation. However, if a person is exhibiting a closed body language and then quickly changes to an open presentation, it exhibits an extreme change in emotion.

If you are talking to a person and they are in a curled up fetal position exhibiting closed body language and then all of a sudden they are sitting up, feet planted on the ground, or spring up to an upright stance, you may have said something that triggered an extreme mood change. At this time, the open body language may not be presenting as relaxed at all but more of an aggressive or defensive body language. Determine quickly what was said that possibly caused the sudden mood swing so that you can direct the conversation in a fashion that does not lead to physical attack.

The Relaxed Body Language

Relaxed body language is when a person's breathing is slower than normal and overall body affect is relaxed without tense muscle tone. Even skin tone color will be normal. Hands, feet and arms are not fidgety or twitching and are laid loosely in their lap or rested. Facial expression is relaxed with a possible slight smile or relaxed mouth. Voice tone is steady with no exaggerated high or low tone fluctuations. The face will be without exaggerated frown lines, the eyes will mimic the mouth; if a slight smile is on the mouth, there will be a slight smile in the eyes and the eyebrows will be at their natural level without tension.

The "I-Am-Boss" Body Language

Power body language is a form of dominant body language but also has a rescue/hero aspect to it as well. People who use power body language on a regular basis are those who are in a position of authority or like to act as if they are. It can be a spouse or partner that tries to remain the power center in a relationship that uses power body language. If a person appears to always have control over your time and space, they are more than likely exhibiting a lot of power play body language and this is one way they have achieved this power over you.

In the business world power is exhibited and acknowledged by the employees starting from the company parking lot. Those in positions of power always have the reserved and best parking spots. This is the beginning of dominating space and exhibiting ones status over another. They display their position and status from the car they drive to the size of the office they sit in, with a door that they can close to allow them the power to select when they want to deal with the hired help. They will take extended lunches but have the hired help punch in and out to ensure they do not over extend the designated time given for lunch breaks.

Power handshakes are one way a person will demonstrate their power over another. Upon greeting, if someone they feel is of lesser status than they are, the power player will give a firm handshake, draw the person in physically, grip the elbow of the arm they are shaking with opposite hand and hold the shake longer then a normal shake. If you want to counteract a power handshake, offer a limp, weak grip. As an extended handshake can make one feel uncomfortable, when exerting a power handshake and receiving a weak limp grip in return, the uncomfortable feeling is turned back on the power player. Power players will hold a gaze longer than normal, another way of making the receiver feel uneasy. Although the gaze is not threatening, it is just enough to make the receiver squirm a bit. The counteraction for a power gaze is to just look away - do not fall for the power play and get into a stare down as breaking the gaze yourself gives you back your personal power. Power players will also dictate where another will sit, gesturing with their hand towards a seat when offering you a chair. Whenever possible, if you want to counteract the power play, choose where and how you will sit before being directed.

If you are meeting a person who is known for power plays, go early and get your seat first. Power players are great at making another wait on them. If there is a planned meeting, you can bet the power player will make everyone wait on them. Other common traits of power body language are invasion of personal space by standing close to another, touching while speaking such as putting a hand on another's shoulder, and an aggressive walk.

The Body Language That Shouts "I'm Ready"

Ready body language is just what it reads. Think of a baseball player in the outfield, their body poised for action – this is ready body language. The body will be turned towards the direction of where the action is taking place or where the perceived action will come from. A teenage girl waiting by the phone to pounce on it when it rings because she is waiting for her boyfriend to call is ready body language. A person eyes will be directed towards where the action is or will come from as well. Their body will be tensed up and ready for action and they may be fidgeting with their hands or twisting on a piece of clothing or another object while waiting in anticipation for the action.

Children show their anxious ready body language when you tell them you will soon be ready to leave to take them to the park or beach. Even if nervous about the action, such as a fight or a student getting ready to do their first solo performance will present with ready body language. Brides waiting to walk down the aisle and grooms waiting for the bride to walk down the aisle are also exhibiting ready body language.

The Body Language of Flirting

Romantic body language is not just what a couple do when they are close and personal but from afar as well and incorporates everything between flirting to marriage and even break ups and divorce.

Body language from afar incorporates all the different forms of flirting one does with their body, from batting eyelashes to how one holds their body to how one even preens and preps to get ready for the occasion of flirting.

Romantic body language from afar can even include sexual gestures. In flirting, looking for a possible long term serious relationship, sexual gestures are not a good idea, however if you are looking to put a little spice back into a marriage, some sexual gesturing body language can be a lot of fun. From afar, romantic body language can be seen from how one display themselves as well. Men and women may wear clothing that accentuates certain parts of their body they find more attractive. Men are notorious for displaying acts of body language when it comes to pumping out certain muscles to make them appear bigger than what they are such as when they cross their arms with their hands under their biceps. If they see someone they are interested in, they can hold a tightened flex forever! Some women tend to hold in their tummy to make it look smaller than what it is and sticking the chest out to make it look larger than what it is.

When using romantic body language from afar, a person will position himself or herself to be in the eye-view of their target of interest by turning their full body or head directly towards them. A person may dance seductively on the dance floor while looking occasionally over to the person they are interested in to make eye contact.

Up close and personal body language should only be done if you are already in a personal relationship with the other party. If you are not in a personal relationship with the other party, you risk having a sexual harassment lawsuit filed against you. Close romantic body language is more intimate than from afar.

A mutual comfort level allows the other to enter into one's personal space without the other feeling threatened. Close romantic body language can exhibit in a couple copying each other's moves or body positions, gazing lovingly into one another's eyes, touching toes while watching TV, holding hands, massages, caressing, kissing, intimate encounters and sexual exploration. Romantic body language when a relationship goes wrong can be a vast mixture between numerous types of body language and is far too complex to cover in this e-book.

The "I'm Listening" Body Language

Attentive body language is the act of showing through body language that you are listening and hearing what another is saying. Yawning or nodding off would be an example of inattentive body language. Being able to properly exhibit attentive body language can make a huge impact if you are applying for a job or are in any field of employment that requires verbal contact with people.

Another situation where having great skills in attentive body language is in personal relationships and intimate situations. Strong attentive body language shows that you have a sincere interest in what another is saying, is flattering, and will most likely result in mutual attention. One way to appear to be actively listening to another through body language is by leaning into the person who is talking, however, respect personal boundaries when doing so. You will be able to tell if a person is listening to you attentively if their gaze is on you and does not reflect away sporadically during the conversation. They will also blink less than normal. Quite often, when a person is attentively listening to another, their frown line will be indented showing that they are concentrating on what you are saying. You will also notice a nodding of the head in agreement or disagreement of things you are saying along with verbal utterances such as "hmmm, uh huh, etc." The person listening may also mimic your body language.

CHAPTER 3- THE NEGATIVE BODY LANGUAGE

The Aggressive Body Language

Aggressive body language is way more than simply punching someone. There are many types of aggressive signals that if picked up on early can save you from being a receiver of a physical attack or give you time to turn the aggression down. Aggressive body language is a signal to a possible physical threat or a verbal threat at the least. As we were taught early on, physical confrontations can never lead to any good so learning to pick up the threat signals early on is extremely beneficial. If you work in a setting where there are volatile people, in a prison setting for example, knowing signals of aggressiveness could even save your life. Aggressive threat body language can come from facial, attack and exposing. Facial signals that can alert you to a possible threat are frowns, pursed lips, reddening of face, sneers, clinched jaw, stare downs with a squint and jerking of head towards you, much like one would jerk their body towards you in an aggressive advancement.

Another common facial threat signal is a person getting right up in your face with their face. With all of these gestures, it is best you step back a couple of feet to put a bit of distance between you and the aggressive person to give you a chance to possibly defuse the situation. The attack stance of body language is typically the positioning of feet for stability and clinching of fist and muscles. There are however some that rarely show little outward physical cues that indicate they are about to punch you. This is when body language alone can put one in a risky situation and it is important to listen to word cues as well.

Another form of aggressive body language is crossing personal space, mental or emotional boundaries. Fake friendships are an example of crossing all three of these boundaries. By pretending to be a friend to another with intent of harm, aggressive body language takes on a chameleon effect; they will use smiles and friendly gestures to gain closeness. Everyone has a comfort zone called his or her personal space and when that is crossed physically (e.g. getting up in someone's face, bumping chest, physically touching another without permission etc.), that invasion of space is an aggressive body language move. People generally do this to get into close proximity of their prey so they can have power over another by making them feel uncomfortable and to make it easier for them to make the first physical strike.

Physical aggressive body language gestures are another indicator that you may be at risk of becoming a victim. Hand gestures are often used to incite another into a physical confrontation, from the use of "flipping someone off" with the flagging of the middle finger, to gang hand signs, thrusting of arms to the ever popular head roll/thrust generally followed with verbal insults. Another obvious great indicator is the mock attacks such as shadow boxing, slamming fist on table (wall, door, etc.), head butting gesture, kicking, etc. without actually making physical contact with you.

The Closed Body Language

Have you ever wondered if your spouse, friend, co-worker or boss was bored with everything that you say but you were not quite able to tell by their body language? Well now, you will be able to tell if what you are saying is falling upon deaf ears. One of the first cues that someone is totally tuning you out is their gaze level. If they are constantly distracted by every little noise or movement, you can bet they are not truly paying attention to you, regardless of how many times they tell you they are listening. A huge clue is when a person begins to yawn or slouch. Granted, yawning can be an indicator that a person is lacking oxygen or is tired however, a person will also yawn when bored. If someone straight up falls asleep on you, then you have a real problem with your presentation skills and should consider taking some speech or affective communication classes. Some reasons people may choose to tune out is that the topic you are discussing with them is something they do not want to listen to or they have heard repeatedly from you before. If a person has no stake in what you are discussing, it is very easy for them to lose interest and become bored quickly. When speaking to a group or on a one to one basis, it is important to use body language while you speak. Facial and hand movements can help to emphasize what you are trying to get across as well as stimulate both the visual and audio senses in your audience. Long drawn out explanations is another quick way to lose your audience attention. Keep it short and to the point - you do not need to re-explain the same thing 50 different ways to get your point across. A good indicator of interest level is to ask questions when speaking with anyone.

Often, if a person is bored you may also see closed body language. Closed body language tells you that your audience has totally shut down on you and as far as they are concerned, you are not even in the same room with them. Teens are excellent examples in using closed body language. This type of body language can also present a defensive action for people as well. If you are confronting a person and they exhibit closed body language, it may be because you are scaring them and in order for you to get across what you are trying to say effectively, you should change your approach. Examples of closed body language are curling up in a ball, rocking, tightly folded arms almost in a self-hug formation, legs tightly crossed or even twisted/intertwined with one another or with a chair or table leg, and a downward gaze or fixated gaze at an object, wall or even feet. There may be many reasons why you receive closed body language from an individual so do not automatically assume it is all about you or what you are saying. The person may have just had an extremely difficult day. When you experience someone who appears to close up during a discussion, note what was being said at the time that the body language changed. It can be a good indicator as to what is possibly going on with them.

When a person feels threatened, even verbally, their body will react. They will get into either a defensive mode or an aggressive mode. In the defensive mode, it is self-preservation. Curling up in a ball protects vulnerable organs and body parts in case of an attack and it can also act as a self-nurturing affect to soothe a person. Another reason people may exhibit closed body language is that they are trying to hide something from the other person such as tears or facial expressions. Ways to move a person from a closed body language to a more open and accepting body language is to offer them something to hold such as a drink, or with a child, a toy. Another way is to mimic their body language, however not in a demeaning manner. Move in closer while still respecting personal space and gradually work into copying their closed body language as this can build a non-verbal bond. As the person begins to relax their closed body position, you also begin to relax at their rate and comfort level.

The Body Language of False Pretense

Deceptive body language should be necessary for everyone to learn. It can help you to distinguish if someone is being honest with you or trying to pull a fast one. Mind you, there are those that are quite good at covering deceptive body language, such as sales people, psychopaths and criminally minded individuals. One common way to tell if a person is being deceptive by their body language is to watch for anxiety cues. Some common anxiety cues are sweating, tension, rubbing the back of the neck or other body parts, sudden movements, body twitches, voice change and increase in speed of speech, chewing on the inside of one's mouth, and shoving hands in pockets or high fidgety. A person when lying will often try to hide their deception by attempting to gain control over their body language through forced smiles and exaggerated hand gestures. This may present as odd, clumsy or jerking movements. Their speech may be hesitated in their attempts to slow it down and thinking intensively as to what to say next. They will often speak looking distracted and avoid eye contact. If standing, they may shift their weight from one foot to another more often than normal as well.

Law enforcement is trained to read body language. As part of that training, they learn about how the brain works and how the body reacts when using different parts of the brain when thinking, such as eye movement. It is believed that the direction one looks when responding to a question can help in determining if the person is lying. This is not always a good indicator to be used in truth finding, however if a person looks to the right while answering a question, you should at least pay close attention to what they are saying. It is thought to be an instinctive action to look to the right when one is utilizing the left side of their brain, the logic and analytic side and to look to the left when using the right side of your brain, the emotional and creative side. It is thought that when a person is lying they utilize the left part of their brain to create the lie which causes their eyes to gaze to the right. There is documentation that states differing views on lying and eye gaze, some say a person is lying when they look to the right whereas others say the left. So do not be judge and jury just because of the direction a person looks when they respond to a question you ask or are telling you a story. Pay close attention to all their body language as well as their words before throwing the book at someone.

Here are a few more interesting things about eye gaze when trying to recall a memory or store data. When we are trying to recall a memory, we use the right side of our brain, making our eyes gaze to the left. When you are seeking visual memories your eyes gaze upward and when a person gazes downward, they are trying to recall emotional memories. However, the shifty eye, gazing right to left does not mean the person is a shyster, it only means they are trying to recall or process auditory memories.

The Defensive Body Language

Defensive body language expresses a person's feeling of physical or emotional threat or personal space being invaded. Automatically when a person feels like they are at risk of physical attack, they cower to protect vital body organs such as curling up in a ball and tucking their head in. Men when faced with an attack by a female almost always aim to protect their groin first. If you even pretend like you are going to strike a man, watch how fast they protect the family jewels by either lifting a leg for protection, or their hands drop to cross in front of their crotch. When face up against another man however, men will generally be in a fending off stance with arms drawn out and jaw/nose region protected. They will harden their muscles in order to withstand an attack better. A common body language signal that will tell you if a woman is uneasy is, if carrying a purse or a bag, the grip will become tighter and it will be drawn in close to their body.

Some people, when uneasy, will display defensive body language by putting a barrier between them and the person or situation that is making them feel uncomfortable. This could be a chair, table, or even holding a package out in front of them making an obstacle between them and the perceived threat. They may grip their keys in between their fingers to use as weapons if a confrontation were to arise. Another defensive body language cue is when someone becomes stiff or rigid. They will attempt to not make a single move with their body to draw attention to themselves while at the opposite side of the spectrum, a person in a defensive mode will scan a room or location for an escape route, or may even flee the room if they perceive the threat level too high. Some individuals, when faced in a possible threatening situation, may never exhibit signs of defensive body language and instead present themselves with either submissive or aggressive body language.

The Dominant Body Language

Dominant body language is closely related to aggressive body language but at a lesser emotional level. The ultimate goal of dominant body language is to impress power over another but not necessarily in an aggressive manner, more so in an authoritative manner.

A person demonstrating dominant body language will often try to make their body appear bigger than what it really is, especially men. Often they will cross their arms with their hands under their biceps in an attempt to push them out more to give a larger appearance. Men and women will hold their hands on their hips with elbows out wide while standing, chest out and chin up. You will see many mothers in this position when disciplining their children.

A great example of using dominant body language over another is a detective over a suspect in an interrogation room. In interrogation rooms, you will often see the detective standing making the suspect sit to give them a dominating height over the suspect in an attempt to intimidate them. The detective may stance the room, much like marking territory designating where exactly the suspect is to sit also while walking around or coming up behind the suspect, leaning over the suspects shoulder to talk rather than sitting at the table with them. By invading the personal space of the suspect they make the suspect feel uncomfortable with the added height and being talked down to, the detective achieves a dominant stance as well as dominance over his territory. The detective makes a point to make sure the suspect knows they are on the detectives' territory and working from the detectives' rules. They will dominate the suspect in other fashions as well, such as cussing and name-calling and having a folder in front of them, leaving the suspect to wonder what type of evidence the detective actually has against them.

Tape recorders, although used in the line of any interrogation, is also another way to non-verbally or non-body language dominate another by leaving the suspect knowing that anything they say is being recorded. You will also see a detective using facial expressions to taunt, control, and dominate the situation. It can be in the form of stare downs, rolling of eyes every time the suspect says something, yawning, squinting at the suspect while holding a stare down, as well as smirking at the suspects' responses.

CHAPTER 4- UNDERSTANDING BODY LANGUAGE THAT IS EITHER POSITIVE OR NEGATIVE

The Emotional Body Language

Emotional body language is a very broad area as a person feels many different emotions. Anger for example displays differently from happy body language, however some body language signals of happy can be mixed up with sad body language. There are many non-verbal signs that can help you to determine what another person is feeling emotionally, however they are not exclusive and no two people necessarily react the same way to the same stimuli. What you would think should make a person sad, may actually not have any effect on another.

Anger can be present in a person for many reasons, such as getting a bad test score, having a bad day at work or a bounced check to numerous other situations. Some things may anger one person deeper than another and/or quicker. Common body language signals of anger are a flushed, red face and/or neck, clenched jaw and/or fist, pacing, invasion of personal space of another with no regards, and the use of aggressive or power body language.

Fear, anxiety and/or nervousness can all present very similar common characteristics in body language. Knowing a bit about the situation while reading the person's body language can help you get a better idea of exactly which of the three emotions they are experiencing. Learning emotional body language is very beneficial in helping a child express in words what their body is feeling. Fear, anxiety and/or nervousness are hard ones for a child to distinguish and can show in a person through their body by breaking out in a cold sweat, paled face, dry mouth, diverting from eye contact or they can appear as they are on the verge of tears. They may exhibit trembling lip, twitching eye, voice tremors, stuttering, cracks in voice, sweating, heightened pulse, clenched fist, muscles and/or jaw and extended periods of holding their breath. Some may present as fidgety while others may take on a defensive or ready body language stance. As you can see, many of these body language signals are also present under other emotions other than fear, anxiety and/or nervousness.

However, as stated before, if you know a little about what is going on, you can generally determine the exact emotion the person is feeling and exhibiting through their body language before even having to speak to them. This is helpful to know if the person fears you or if they are just nervous about the situation or having anxiety about it. It will help you to put the person at ease better in order to come to some sort of resolution.

Sadness body language generally presents with slouching or drooping of the shoulders or body, almost limp like, possible trembling lip, tears, and a flat speech tone. Embarrassment can present with a red face, avoidance of eye contact, grimaced face or a meek smile and can also cause withdrawal in some people.

Surprised body language will present with the widening of the eyes and raised eyebrows. Emotional body language expressing happiness can present in tears of joy, smiling mouth and eyes and an overall relaxed demur. Extreme happiness may present with a person doing what is known as the happy dance where they are jumping around. Although all of these are very common types of body language used to express emotion, a person with a flat affect may not show any of these. They could be extremely happy and only show it with a slight smile, if that.

Body Language that Suggests Careful Thinking

Evaluating body language is how a person uses their body when evaluating a situation. This could present in hand movements when discussing how a back yard deck design should go, or on a determination of which direction one should turn while driving. People who generally do a lot of talking with hand gestures will exhibit a large amount of body language when evaluating or thinking about something as well.

Another form of evaluating body language is the formation of sorts similar to that of praying hands while thinking. They may tap a finger on their chin or even rub their chin; their lips may purse and for those you encounter that wear eyeglasses, you may notice that while evaluating a situation that they peer over the top of them when in discussion rather than through them. Professors, teachers, and doctors who wear eyeglasses are known for this. Generally, their body will present relaxed and comfortable although they are concentrating intensely.

Ronald Young

The Body Language of a Lioness

Submissive body language should not be mistaken for passive body language and exhibits conquered as well as being used to signal fear. Think of a lion taking a lioness; at first the lioness will fight the lions attempt to subdue her and eventually the lioness submits. She cowers to his aggression and allows the lion to take her. That is submissive body language in the form of conquered.

In the form of signaling fear, a person may cower into a fetal position or exhibit closed body language until the perceived threat has passed. Some specific submissive body language signals one may notice are the holding of the head down avoiding eye contact with others while in public, widening of eyes to appear more innocent, much like the bright wide eyes of an infant and attentively looking into the eyes of someone who is speaking to them that is their dominant. A submissive person will exchange in conversation of someone more dominant than themselves but generally they will always agree with them. They will make eye contact with a dominant and smile; however, their smile will be subdued.

Women tend to exhibit more submissive body language then men. Men, however have a misplaced train of thought when they think that some cultures of women are submissive by nature such as Asian women. Asian women are not any more submissive than any other women; their culture is different and they value their family and pride themselves in being a great wife and mother. This by no means makes her submissive.

Chapter 5- Decoding Lies

People lie for a variety of reasons. It may be to cover up a fault or embarrassment, to avoid upsetting other people, to encourage when no hope can be perceived, or to be spared from petty hassles. It may also be due to more serious psychological problems such as delusional imaging or extreme vanity.

Here are some indications that are conveyed by people when lying:

•They speak in a high-pitched, fast-paced, stuttering voice.

•They are constantly swallowing and clearing their throat.

•They try their best to avoid having eye contact. This applies particularly to people who want to avoid discussing a certain topic.

•They stick their tongue out to moist their lips.

•They are blinking rapidly.

•They rub their throat.

•Their arms are crossed over the chest.

•They are constantly touching parts of their face, especially the mouth, ear, and nose as if covering them.

•They scratch their head or the back of the neck.

•Their poses are closed, descending, and insecure.

•Their hands or feet are tapping.

•They always look down with shrugged shoulders.

•They are constantly moving from one place to another or changing their poses.

•They are projecting parts of their body (feet) to an escape route

Every person has a unique body language. Although silence usually denotes that an individual is reserved and relaxed, some people keep their anger within themselves and stay quiet. (This is very unhealthy because rage kept up inside can explode furiously anytime, causing serious casualties). A wide open mouth may indicate shock or astonishment for one person, while another person who performs this gesture could just be concentrating intently on a task he's doing. Constantly touching the mouth may indicate lying, although the real reason might just be that the mouth is itching.

One way to overcome this dilemma is to watch out for other signals that jive with the body language being exhibited. For example, you can confirm if a person is really nervous if he exhibits many of the qualities of nervousness described above. Judgment based on one or two gestures only may not be accurate enough, although they can be dependable. Be aware of the body language, but also combine your observations with the spoken words to get more hints regarding the inner feelings of another. Use this power to your advantage.

Chapter 6- Mirroring Body Language Styles from Surrounding People

Who would you rather be with? Your best friend who loves pizza as much as you do, who's crazy about basketball like you are, who watches the same programs on TV as you; or your next-door neighbor who's a vegetarian, hates sports, and watches those shows that will bore you to dreamland?

The answer is obvious. You would want to be around people who have the same behaviors, attitudes, and values as yours. Birds of the same feather flock together. Bookworms like each other's company because they share a common bond - their love for books. Basketball fanatics flock together because they can RELATE to each other's interests and ideas. If you really want someone to like and trust you, you've got to exhibit the same qualities as that person. And there's no better way to do this than by using body language.

Here's how it goes:

Match their facial expressions, gestures, posture, speech, styles, and actions, breathing patterns, values and beliefs. Put yourself in their shoes. In other words, BE THEM. By doing this, you are also matching their way of thinking. You may easily adapt to their inner thoughts and views. You may also do some crossover matching. For example, you talk at the same rate as their breathing. Or you can scratch your chin every time their eyes blink. Get the idea?

Be genuinely interested and curious with everything you can find out about them. Discover their attitude. Know their life story. This is what we call mirroring. But mirroring should not be confused with mimicry. You should act with courtesy and caution. Never let the person you're mirroring be aware of what you're doing. Just imagine acting out shamelessly what the other person is doing. Every time he stands, you stand. When he scratches his head, you also scratch your head. That would be insulting. Never let the person you're mirroring have any chance to think that you are mocking him. Your main objective should be to influence the subconscious. Even if a person is not aware that you're mirroring him, his subconscious mind realizes it. The person will subconsciously be at ease when you duplicate his manners indirectly. He will feel very comfortable if you're both on the same level.

Matching Body Language with the Other Person's Mood

If you're mirroring a person who has lots of problems, don't come to him in a joyous mood and say, "Don't worry about it. Let's watch a movie so that you'll forget about whatever's bugging you." He's in a foul mood. He expects you to feel for him, to empathize with him. Match his disposition first, and then say something like, "I feel bad for you. If there's anything I can do to help, just let me know."

All he wants right now is to be with someone who has the same mood as he has. A word of warning though, if someone has some really big emotional problems, and you mirror that person, you run the risk of actually absorbing his emotions. So do this activity in a low-risk situation.

Rapport – The Ultimate Goal of Body Language

The ultimate goal of mirroring is to build rapport. It's the time when you and the people you're mirroring feel so close and in synch with each other that you feel like you've known each other for years. So how would you know if you've built rapport? Mirror them. Match whatever characteristic, value, or behavior they possess that you would like to copy. After some time, touch your nose or cross your legs. If they do the same thing, mission accomplished! You've already lowered their defenses to the point where they are more receptive to your suggestions. You can even build rapport even if a person you're mirroring is far away. Here's how to do it:

1. Just relax. Clear your mind of all negative thoughts and create a bond by focusing on the entire body of the person you wish to mirror. Make his image so real and vivid.

2. Use your subconscious to enter his world. Feel the connection. Give out positive projections uniting his entire persona into yours.

3. Think of what he may be doing at the moment. Then replicate his actions, behaviors, and principles.

With this exercise, you can even emulate your role models. Let's say you want to be as successful as your boss who is always traveling around the world. Do the above exercise and you'll soon see some astounding results.

Chapter 7- Body Language in Negotiating Tables

In almost every point in your life, you unconsciously do the art of negotiations. From haggling with your favorite flea market sales lady, to lobbying for a well-deserved increase from your boss, negotiations are being made daily in your life. And would you believe almost all aspects of the negotiation process involves body language? In terms of the actual negotiation in business, body language is a very important aspect. Reading body movements of your counterparts and making the right gestures may spell the difference between success and failure in the negotiation process.

How Do You Act When Entering the Negotiating Room?

The first step in using body language in a negotiation begins the moment you walk into the negotiation room. Be keen in observing their body language by focusing on the whole body - the head, arms, hands, chest, tummy, legs and feet. If you achieve this, you will be able to listen better. You will also be more perceptive in reading their body language.

Invading Personal Space Might Jeopardize Negotiations

In the negotiating table, each person creates his own personal space, his own territory. By business practice, people of higher status (e.g. president of a company) command more personal space, and are usually conferred by other people in the negotiating table. For example, the authority over the most dominant chair (usually the head of the table) is the apparent symbol of power. If this person occupies the dominant chair, a good negotiator can repel this by strategic seating arrangement of teams or allies in the negotiating table. Surround that person in a seating arrangement where you may comfortably get leverage.

The Very Crucial First Move

In the negotiating table, the first move is the most crucial. Just like in the game of chess, if you play the white piece, you get the built-in advantage because you draw first blood, and the opponent's next move and game plan for that matter is dependent on that crucial first move. So make a good, firm, and calculated move. Begin with a positive body language. Radiate your enthusiasm. In a meeting for example, look in the other person's eyes with sincerity. Your eyes are the windows to your soul. If you can't maintain eye contact, they might think you're hiding something or you're not sincere.

Give a solid handshake. Hold the hand firmly but don't squeeze it. A common fallacy is that we should squeeze the hand during this monumental time of the handshake. This is certainly not advisable. Press the hand one time while looking the person straight in the eye. Pressing the hand once or twice may indicate excitement or vitality, but anything more than that can make the other person uneasy. During the negotiation process, observe their gestures.

In the first chapter, you were taught how to determine if people are interested in what you are saying; if they are casting doubts on you; if they are more open to accept your proposal; and even when they are lying. Be alert in recognizing these signals. Moreover, also be aware of your own actions. You might be exhibiting signs of nervousness without you knowing it, and your counterparts (who might also know body language) might take advantage of the circumstances.

Chapter 8- How Body Language is Used in Selling

Studies in Psychology tell us that the effect you have on others depends on what you say from the mouth (7%), the manner in which you say it (38%), and by your body language (55%). In addition, how you sound also imparts a message, so 93% of emotion is also conveyed without saying the actual words. This is also true in selling. In the real world, we sell tangible items and also ideas.

A concise way on how we can sell effectively is by simply using that old but very powerful arsenal known as body language. When you sell, you can use postures, facial expressions, gestures, mannerisms, and your physical appearance to close the sale successfully. Most customers tend to buy when triggered by their senses. The key here is to do everything you can to positively affect their senses.

Most people believed the image projected by Saint Mother Theresa is a positive image. She used her personality to convey a constant image of holiness and sincerity. We bought the idea of her image. Non-verbal communication also connotes that a man of few words is a man of credibility. It's often not what you say that influences others; it's what you don't say. The signals that you impart using body movements suggest comprehension, disposition, morality, and compassion.

In selling, the instant you meet a target client, he is already examining you based on your image and perception in a span of ten seconds or less. This is a crucial moment in selling, as his first impression of you will definitely make a permanent mark. Whether you make or break a sale can literally depend on the non-verbal signals that you send during this crucial first contact. It's a must for readers of this book to understand the facets of body language especially in selling. Americans, for example, are somewhat categorized as one of the best in reading body language, because they espouse thousands of non-verbal signs. This ability makes them formidable negotiators. In addition, women are generally considered to be more adept to body language than men because of their natural built-in instincts. Now you know the secret why some women are more successful than men in the business or professional field.

As a rule of thumb, body language is being used most of the time all over the world. The most common example is a nodding head (meaning "yes"). But it is not necessarily the case every time. For example, shaking legs might connote that a person is nervous, while it may just be a person's natural behavior. A person's eyes could evade you because he's hiding something, or it could also mean that he's extremely shy. Given these intricacies, what's important is to analyze what the message really is.

You can do it by looking at patterns. Look out for groups of signals that may have the same meaning in relation to the verbal expressions, and also in cognizance to the circumstances. Once you have traced the patterns, it is easier to understand body language. It will therefore help you make a sale.

Written below are some body language techniques to help make your sales sizzle:

1. You can immediately analyze a person's personality by studying his style in shaking hands. An assertive person holds your hand firmly when you shake his hand. On the other hand, an individual with little or no confidence often gives a frail handshake. A person who wants to win your trust would usually shake your hand with his other hand covering the shake or holding your elbow. Adopt a handshake that is firm, yet not crushing. Convey confidence and professionalism, not dominance.

2. Posture is another aspect of body language. A slouching shoulder with your eyes looking on the ground can indicate lack of interest. Standing straight with your weight balanced on each foot gives you a more assured and relaxed look. Always maintain a straight body, whether you're standing or sitting.

3. Match the straight open posture with a genuine facial expression. Dispose of the sunglasses. The client may think that you are hiding something, as he can't see through your eyes. When he looks straight in your eyes, he can tell if you are lying, so be transparent. Lay down your cards and throw the shades away. But be sure to avoid piercing looks. The client might get intimidated.

4. When doing sales calls and presentations, be sure to use sincere and open movements all the time. Do not cross your arms, as this can ruin the trust of your potential customer. The outward and upward gestures of your hands are recommendable. If you lean back on a chair and place your hands at the back of your head, it

may drive your clients away as this is a sure sign of arrogance and a false sense of confidence. Meanwhile, if you place your hands on your waists, you are exuding positive confidence.

5. "Don't point." Pointing at a client is equivalent to death wish in selling. It is as if you're waving your sales opportunity goodbye. Pointing is an aggressive act that can be interpreted as hostility, so throw this gesture out the window if you really want to sell.

6. In sales, here are signs that you are open for negotiations and are willing to compromise. Unbuttoning your jacket means you are ready to talk and to listen to a counter offer. Removing your jacket or rolling your sleeves up is a very good sign for the client, as this means you are ready to decide or to give in to the final price.

You, as the seller, may also use body language as a tool to recognize and counteract any potential objections by the client.

The usual scenarios include the following:

1. If the client's arms are crossed, it means he is disinterested. Use counter measures like positive movements to cause them to uncross their arms, and for you to begin the sales approach. When his arms and legs are uncrossed, and his hands are open, this is the best scenario, as they are open to your ideas...and a sale is more likely to happen.

2. Another good sales scenario is when the client mimics your gestures like when you fix your hair and the client follows. It shows he is very receptive to your ideas and open to buy your idea or product. If this is the case, throw all your barrage of features and benefits, and close the sale! This point is crucial as you can make or break the sale.

3. If the client covers his mouth, touches his nose, or the part near the eye, there's a probability that you are losing the sale. Something you said or did might have discouraged him. But don't despair. Do the selling process again; but this time, do it differently. Reassure the client that he is getting a great deal and encourage him to open up and share ideas. Open your palms and unconsciously let him see you occasionally putting your palm to your chest (this signifies honesty). Then try to reach that positive sales atmosphere again and close the sale.

4. Always be alert to the signs the client is exhibiting. If the client shows interest through his body movements, give the final sales blow and close the sale. The client's body language may change from positive to suspecting. In this case, take it easy, gather your wits, read your client's moods, and try to win him back. When the client crosses his legs and arms, this is a warning signal. Use mirroring techniques (discussed in the previous chapter). You must make every effort to earn the trust of the client, so that you ultimately can close the deal.

5. In worse cases where you are unable to close the sale, try to be professional and diplomatic at all times. Thank the client for listening and shake his hand with sincerity. Sales cannot be achieved overnight and you generally win some and lose some. Closing the presentation on a positive note will leave a good impression of you. Who knows, he might be your next positive client at some other time. Use your body every way you can in the selling process. Always be enthusiastic. If you truly believe in the high quality of your product or service, other people will be positively affected by your enthusiasm. Body movements can convince prospects to become believers in what you are offering.

Chapter 9- Getting the Job with the Right Body Language

Gone are the days when the job seeker has to write the handwritten application letter to earn that job interview. In this age of computers and cyber technology, most employers prefer applicants who apply online, and more job seekers are looking to the net for their job opportunities. But one thing remains the same - the body language of the applicant during job interviews and how they make the first impression as they step inside that interview room.

What is Your Personality Type?

Based on your body language, an interviewer may know whether you are confident or not, if you are the shy type or the friendly type, if you are a loner or a team player, or even if you are telling the truth or not. They can tell if you are capable of handling the job, if you are devoted, or if you're someone who can get along with other employees. Based on their questions, the interviewer will not only pay attention to what you say, but also on how you say it. The interviewer generally will find responses from you that match their qualifications. How you can decode the body language of your interviewer in relation to your own body language will determine the thin line if you get that job or not.

Be Punctual

This is the most important aspect of the job interview – arriving on time. The job interview is deemed as a very important appointment, and being late is a cardinal crime with gravity that may cause you to lose that job opportunity. Your attitude regarding time will send the wrong messages to the employer, and will tell a lot about your lack of professionalism. Being stuck in traffic is a very lame and downright unforgivable excuse. It is better to be early by one hour than to be a minute late.

The First Encounter

When the interviewer comes to the room to meet you, do not offer your hand for a handshake unless the interviewer offers his hand. Shake hands firmly, but do not squeeze. Maintain eye contact.

Proper Body Posture

Body posture is important during job interviews and you can adopt the following stance. At the beginning of the interview, sit up straight in your chair, with your back leaning against the back of the chair. Do not slouch or move sideways in your chair because it might be perceived by the interviewer as a lack of interest or boredom. On the other hand, sitting on the edge of your chair can impart a message that you are a little nervous and that you feel uneasy with the situation. When the interviewer says something, it is advisable to lean forward a little. This shows interest and attention in what the interviewer is saying. You can tilt your head a little to show that you are listening closely.

Proper Gestures

Do not cross your arms because this might be perceived as a defensive move. Just place your hands loosely on your lap or just put them on the armrest of your chair. By doing this, you will also be able to make hand movements to support what you are saying. While speaking, you may nod your head occasionally to expound on a subject or to give more meaning to what you are saying. Hand movements can also help to spice up the conversation. The interviewer would think that you are comfortable with the interview process if you make hand gestures.

Too much hand movements at the beginning of the interview may not be a good idea. The proper way is to add them gradually throughout the interview. Be aware of your interviewer's hand movements as well. If they use their hands a lot to make a point or to clarify something, you can do the same thing as well (Remember mirroring?). When they don't make many movements, do the same thing as them. It is important to adjust your gestures to that of the interviewer to establish rapport. Be alert to unintentional gestures that you may make sometimes due to tension.

Some of the acts that may irritate the interviewer could include:

•Tapping your fingers on the desk.

•Shuffling your feet.

•Biting your nails.

•Toying with a pen.

The Panel Interview

Being interviewed by one person could be a piece of cake for many. But being interviewed by a group could be a confusing ordeal, especially when it comes to who you should look at during the interview. It is important to maintain eye contact with all the interviewers at an equal extent. By looking uniformly at them, you will establish their trust and you will gain composure throughout the interview process. When one of the interview partners asks or says something, maintain eye contact with him until he ceases speaking. This will indicate that you're listening attentively. While he is speaking, he may also look at the other interviewers. When he looks at you again, you can nod your head to encourage him to continue speaking. When you answer a question, look first at the one who asked. But while you are answering, you should take turns looking at each of the other interviewers as well. You should direct yourself again to the person who asked the question when you want to prove a point, when you want to emphasize something, and when you are done answering.

Body Language of Your Interviewers

Observing the body language of your interviewers is as important as being aware of your own body movements. The body gestures of your interviewers can give you an indication of how well you are coming across to them. This can serve as a signal to change your approach at an early stage before they give you the thumbs down. For example, when you did something that displeases the interviewers, they will show their annoyance through body language. When they sigh, shake their heads, look down, or fold their arms and lean back, you can take this as a sign of discontentment or irritability. The interviewers might not consciously notice that they're exhibiting their body movements at first, so you still have a chance to shift your strategy.

It's Okay to be Nervous

Knowing how to act confidently using body language can increase your chances of passing the interview. You can utilize this knowledge to conceal your anxiety a little, but this is something you shouldn't worry about too much. Many applicants are tensed during an interview, and they would not want to let the interviewer know about their inner feelings. However, it is completely understandable to be nervous at this stage. It is completely normal. Your nervousness may even indicate how valuable getting this job is to you. If you weren't nervous, and you act like a happy-go-lucky person, you might be perceived as someone who is not very interested in the job.

The interview not only functions as a way of determining who among the applicants is most capable of performing the job well, but it is also a means of allowing the interviewer to get to know more about the applicants. It's a first encounter with an individual that you might soon work together with. If that's the case, then the interviewer (who could be your boss) should actually feel the same way as you are. Nervousness often accompanies excitement.

Chapter 10- Using Effective Body Language to Set the Image You Want

Most people come to a point in life when they desire to make a complete change to project a new image. After being the old out dated image for so long and finding only boring lifestyle to suit it, the idea of change is more than welcome.

In order to do this rebranding exercise on one's self there has to be a certain clear cut goal to work towards. This is to ensure that the exercise is completed to the end and successfully. Some of the areas worth exploring are personal style, choice of clothing, personal body conditions are just a few to mention.

Changing the personal style of an individual is almost always the first goal to achieve in an overall make over. The general habitual body language should be able to be complimented with the change or adjustment of the personal style.

Having a good personal style will eventually transcend into the ability to make eye contact confidently and thus further portray the confidence in the body language too.

The overall dressing of an individual is also linked to the personality and body language practiced. People who generally prefer to be casually dressed give the impression of being easy going when coupled with the corresponding body language of a much laid back demeanor.

In contrast those who are always impeccably dressed have a rather stiff body language. If the idea is to be more professional in demeanor than the corresponding image should also project this.

For some, the original habit of poor grooming is a norm. If there is to be some form of interaction with others especially in a more friendly way then the issue of personal grooming should be addressed.

Having an image in mind of the desired outcome is the first step to actually considering and changing the overall demeanor of the individual through new and more appropriate body language signals.

Training for Positive Modus Operandi

As already firmly established, body language is a very important stubble form of communicating feelings and reactions to the surroundings. Also previously established is the fact that body language can also be manipulated to an advantage or required circumstances.

Here are some areas where one can train or manipulate the body to react in a certain way in order to achieve the desired results.

• Eye contact – this is an important aspect to be mastered when dealing with people. Ensuring constant eye contact allows the recipient to be assured that there is some level of interest in what is being discussed. Whether feigned or not eye contact is something worth learning to exercise. It also makes the recipient feel more at ease and confident in the situation.

• Poor posture encourages a feeling of tiredness and even reinforces that people to other people. This is due to the hunched or droopy shoulders as well as the hunched positions all contributing to the inhibition of good and deep breathing. This in turn will give the impression of being uncomfortable or nervous.

• Using the head positions to dictate the perceived body language message is also another effective way of making a situation comfortable or uncomfortable. Tilting the head slightly while talking or listening implies a friendly demeanor while keeping the head ramrod straight and aligned with the back and spine implies seriousness and even annoyance.

• The all popular crossing of arms clearly indicates disapproval from time beginning. Commonly done from an authoritative position it tells everyone to back off and give the individual space. On the other hand, hands hanging loosely or kept behind the back implies being in control and able to take on anything, which is a good body language to develop to project the desired effects.

Chapter 11 - Winning a Battle With Non-Verbal Cues

Sometimes when verbal communication does not work, one has to find other alternatives to get the message across effectively and quickly. Everyone has their own distinct ways of expressing themselves and those who are familiar with the body language signs will have no problems interpreting these signals.

In order to create a comfortable situation or improve an otherwise uncomfortable situation the use d of different body language positions can help. These various positions are used to create the desired difference in how people receive the implied messages, the general mood of the recipient or even to strike a balance in those around.

Some commonly practiced and recommended body positions that can help keep those around feeling at ease and even happier are as follows:

• Smiling – this very rarely brings on a negative response or reaction. Most people will almost immediately change their negative responding reaction to a positive one, when a smile is offered. It would be hard to respond to a smile with a harsh negative reaction.

• A confident sitting position is also another way to "shake" any negative elements in both the individual and those around. Giving the impression of being relaxed yet with a certain amount of alertness, the individual will be able to defuse any possible responsive slouching individuals. It also encourages those around to be an energetic as possible with the straight upright position.

• In practicing slower and more precise moments the individual is also creating a sense of calmness all around. This in turn will also encourage those around to be equally calm and relaxed.

All these when put into practice regularly until it becomes fairly natural will cause those around to be positively affected too. When this is accomplished the percentage of confrontations is lessoned and kept under control.

What if You Intentionally Misuse Body Language?

Most people breeze through the day without this reality ever coming the light. However for the discerning and some would sad intelligently scheming few, the purposeful use of body language in the daily life has proven to be quite an effective and beneficial tool.

Practicing to be consciously and continually aware of this sometimes very effective tool is an art worth exploring. However on the other hand the wrong or subconscious use of the body language tool can bring about unnecessary and sometimes annoying results. Incorrect use of body language can bring about the reactions and reflections that are not needed or wanted and thus causing a great inconvenience to both the person suing the body language too and the perceived receiver. Such misinterpretation can end up causing the almost opposite intended reactions.

Especially in relationships when a particularly innocently termed body language is exercised and reflected the consequences of said actions can and often are wrongly perceived, resulting in the very messy process of trying the "straighten" everything out. In business too, a wrong perception of the body language tool can cause very damaging results indeed. Therefore it is indeed prudent to practice to be ever conscious of the body language being implied and practiced. This is indeed necessary to avoid any unnecessary inconveniences from occurring.

About The Author

Ronald holds a degree in Psychology. Formal education and his years as a therapist have honed his people skills and his ability to read non-verbal cues from other people.

Willing to share his ideas to the world, Ronald started writing. This will be his first published work.

www.ingramcontent.com/pod-product-compliance
Lightning Source LLC
Chambersburg PA
CBHW070050260726
48658CB00002B/831